WHITE TIME

TIME

Consciousness Raising Information
For Humanity's Dimensional Shift

KRISTAR

ISBN: 978-0-615-15865-5

1. Metaphysical, non-fiction 2. Spirituality 3. Philosophy
4. Paranormal 5. Poetry

KILLIAN PUBLISHING
621 State Road 9 Ste 3
PMB D-20
Lake Stevens, Wa. 98258

e-mail   s.kristar@yahoo.com

First Edition, Published 2007

DEDICATION

This book is dedicated with love to my family: my daughters, parents, sisters, brothers and grandparents. You have all been my teachers and have helped me greatly along the way.

THANK YOU

The persons listed below I consider to be courageous pioneers who are opening new pathways for humanity on this frontier of raised consciousness. Their work, their books and their teachings have meant a great deal to me as, I am sure, they have to many millions of others. The ideas I put forth are strictly my own. I'm not saying the following people agree with me and I do not agree with all of their ideas. I understand some of them have suffered for their efforts to bring spiritual and paranormal knowledge to public attention. These are brave men and women. As of this writing they all have websites on the internet. Thank you: Gregg Braden (writer, lecturer, researcher), Eckhardt Tolle (writer, teacher), Linda Moulton Howe (writer, journalist, explorer), Art Bell (talk show host, writer), Judith Orloff , M.D. (intuitive, psychiatrist, writer), Whitley Strieber (talk show host, writer, lecturer), Steven Greer, M.D. (Disclosure Project, researcher, writer), Solara (11:11, visionary, writer), George Noory (talk show host, writer), Deepak Chopra, M.D. (Chopra Center, writer, lecturer), Gary Schwartz, PhD (Professor, scientist, writer).

A WORD TO THE READERS

There are many exciting and positive changes happening in our world which I did not have the time, space or inclination to write about. Some of them include; natural healing methods with herbs and energy work; the growing availability of organic foods; the development of alternative energy sources and more people working to protect and repair our earth's environment. Also, there are relatively new and interesting ideas and happenings which invite further research. The following subjects may also be a part of the expansion of consciousness; chaos theory; fractals; crop circles and sacred geometry.

My thanks to the kind people who read this book at my request before publication. Their critiques and feedback were invaluable to me. One critique was that I was ignoring all the terrible and negative things in the world. I do suffer from the knowledge of such things as wars, pollution, starvation, crime, the excessive drugging of America's children and the movement to implant chips in all humanity. Considering there have been animal deaths due to cancerous tumors growing around the animals' implanted chips, this movement may have slowed some. Anyway, my response to this critique was since we are practically swimming in an ocean of negativity, thanks partly to the public media, I didn't need to write about it here. Also, it didn't fit with the purposes of this book which I will mention later on.

A second critique was perhaps some readers would wonder

if waking up to an awareness of our multidimensional selves, and there are more of us doing it every day, was related to a multiple personality disorder. To my knowledge that suggestion and the debate surrounding it are approximately twenty five or thirty years old and have no relevance in today's world, but I will address it here. Currently, there is widespread acceptance of the many dimensions theory due to quantum physics. For myself, and many others I have personally talked with, the awareness of what appears to be other selves in other dimensions consists of fleeting glimpses and/or very brief interactions with other worldly beings. This awareness has not affected our lives except for a cautious consideration of other realities There are a few people who say they have ongoing contact with helpful other dimensional selves. In contrast, multiple personality disorder, which is now called dissociative identity disorder (DID) by the DSM-IV-TR is a serious mental condition often caused by childhood trauma and adversely affects a person's ability to function. Knowledgeable, thinking people see the two as completely separate and unrelated.

My hope is the writings in this book will serve several purposes. One purpose is to help the readers wake up, look around, think, research and participate in their own consciousness raising. Another purpose is to give the readers information with which to deal with possible future events. Still another purpose is to emphasize there is no death, only change, transformation and new beginnings.

KRISTAR

TABLE OF CONTENTS

SECTION I

SECTION II

SECTION III

SECTION I

**DIAMOND PATTERNS
ON TEXTURED GLASS**

WHITE TIME

Blending all the rainbow colors is white light.

Blending future, past and present is white time

And creates the perfect moment of the now.

When we stop the ever marching of the years

And we stop the ever ticking of the clock;

We find the sacred stillness of white time.

That inner place where possibilities exist.

Do we co-create the universe this time

When we dwell in the realm of higher mind?

And we revel in the beauty of white time

In the silent, perfect moment of the now.

QUICKENING

Awakening, awakening,
Sleep has gone away.
Awakening, awakening,
Into a lighter day.
The fascination with limitation
And materialization fades away.
The sanctity of the entity
That knows its' own integrity
Is now the true reality.
  And the force is with us now.
  And the force is with us now.

A quickening, a quickening,
The pace accelerates.
A quickening, a quickening,
Don't be one who hesitates
When the love reverberates.
Positivity facilitates,
Creativity initiates
A faster process now.
  And the force is with us now.
  And the force is with us now.

Cooperation brings synchronization
And affirmation that the vibration
Is higher all the time.
And it's fine, it's just fine.
The vortex of energy moves
The entity past polarity

To the synergy of totality.
Move in wholeness now.
Move in oneness now.
  And the force is with us now.
  And the force is with us now.

A remembering, A remembering,
An evolution of love.
A remembering, a remembering,
A message from above.
The capacity of the entity
To love unconditionally
Is reality of ecstasy.
And love is here to stay.
And love is here to stay.
  And the force is with us now.
  And the force is with us now.

There's very little tension
In the fifth dimension.
Which is the direction
And the reflection
Of our perfection.
Move in wholeness now.
Move in oneness now.
  And the force is with us now.
  And the force is with us now.

TRANSMUTATION

This experiment in matter
Has gotten out of hand.
Much too heavy for us;
Time to take a stand.

We were looking for
New life forms to explore.
Now the pain's too great;
Must learn to transmutate.
But this is where we stay
'Till we lighten up the clay.

We will dance with electrons
When we cross over the bridge.
We'll be good and whole and real;
We'll be made of golden steel.
And we'll claim our birthright
Of love and diamond light.

Don't let the changes get you down.
We've been found; we're upward bound;
Coming round to sacred ground.
It's a joining, a rejoining;
A melding and a welding
Of diamond light and golden steel.

Let's end this experiment right.
Let's change everything to light.
The transmutation of man
Will be a perfect birth.
The transmutation of earth
Will be a crystal birth.

SYMPHONY

Listen well, can you hear
Gentle whispers in the air?
Music stirring everywhere;
Building to crescendo there.
The symphony of the universe
Comes to us, comes to us.

Colors and sounds are blending.
In concert they are sending
Bright harmonics of a golden hue.
Hear the flutes blowing true.
Hear the cymbals crashing through,
Tuneful palettes winging true.

Colors and sounds are mingling.
The cosmic wind is singing.
The symphony of sound and light
Flows through the galaxy bright.
Pulsing beams from starlight
Plays the concert of the night.

In our spirits, the music plays,
Bringing peace throughout the days.
The crystal sounds of the galaxy
From the dawning of infinity
Is eternal music of elation
And sings for us a new creation

QUARKS

Quarks are fundamental units of matter
Subatomic particles

Whirling with neutrons and protons in the atom
They spin through the unified field
Of non locality and quantum possibilities
Turning energy into matter

Are quarks also the points of light
In the matrix

Of the consciousness of the mind of God
Which may be the oneness of the ground of being
Are quarks the building blocks of the universe

Does He image and shape those swirling
Points of light

Into the solid forms He chooses
For His creation

Is that what makes Him
The Master Builder

CAT

I am part mountain cat
And very, very proud of that.
The cat in me wants out;
It wants to leap about.
The cat in me wants out;
Of that there is no doubt.

I did prowl mountains high
And I still feel the thrill
Of jagged peaks against the sky.
The wildness is in me still.
I am cat, hear me roar
Of past nobility.
Before the closing of the door,
It was the time of the cat;
It was the time of the cat.

Memories come of ancient days.
We gathered in the dreamtime ways
To play the games that man,
Now does not understand.
Magic games of Merlin's time
When cat and humankind
Knew the telepathic refrain.
And will we ever regain
That true communication?

I am part mountain cat
And very, very proud of that.
The cat in me wants out;
It wants to leap about.
The cat in me wants out;
Of that there is no doubt.

INBREATH

A pulling from the source;
We feel the tension, too.
A longing from the source;
A yearning in us, true.
A calling from the source;
Perhaps it's nothing new.

Ancient melodramas
Play out again this time.
Ancient cosmic cycles
Are moving us in line.
The inbreath of the source
Is opening our mind.

When source breathed out before
Were we abandoned then?
Was it always known
The pathway we would wend
Until there was a sign?
Outward journey's at an end.

And should we willing go
Or do we fight the trend
As source recalls us now?
Since we have had to fend
For ourselves a time
Should we protest the end?

We study ancient lore.
Little was known in full.
We don't resist the tide
And slip into a lull.
Then we let go of pride
And surrender to the pull.

MULTIDIMENSIONAL ENTITY

It's a strange old universe,
But it's the only game in town.
A fascinating theory
Seems to be a coming down.
You're a multidimensional entity;
There's more of you around.

Did they tell you guys and gals?
We seem to have lots of pals
From the future and the past.
Lighter dimensions are coming fast.
A parallel universe closes down,
From there another self is found.

Laughter is your best defense.
Makes us lighter, not so dense.
Laughter heals the wounds of time.
A light vibration is just fine.
You have many playmates, true.
There are many parts of you.

You're a multidimensional entity,
Not a multiple personality.
So if you sing a silly tune
They won't call you a loon.
Won't lock you in a room
'Cause you laugh at your own silly tune.

Laughter is your best defense.
Makes us lighter, not so dense.
Blending selves can be fun;
Joining to a wholesome one.
Integration can be fun
When we know the final one.

Let's keep the human identity
In the completed entity.
Laughter blends the selves in time.
A lighter vibration is just fine.
Laughter is your best defense.
Makes us lighter, not so dense.

CROP CIRCLES

Circles and designs in cereal crops
Have been seen all around the world.
Are they the language of sacred geometry?
Those mathematical shapes and solids
That are the building blocks of the universe.

Are the pictographs messages to us?
If so, the code is most obscure.
Are they date markers for time travelers?
Some people say they may be directions
For humanity to build a starship
Or an inter-dimensional portal.

What little we seem to know
Shows they are formed by energy,
In seconds or minutes of time.
Perhaps it's microwave energy
Directed from an orbiting satellite.

Are there ancient keepers who hold
The form of earth in their consciousness?
And, when needed, send streaming energy
To keep Gaia's natural patterns intact.
To repair the wear and tear and damage
Inflicted on our beautiful earth.

Is the energy being made visible now
In sacred, geometrical designs
To make us wonder, to wake us up?
So we can cooperate with the keepers
In restoring our beloved mother earth.

LIFE

New life is always beautiful.
Incredible, wonderful,
Procreating, propagating,
Replicating, duplicating,
Generating, celebrating,
Life, life, life.

New life is always precious,
Joyous, sensuous, delicious.
Now open your heart to seeing
The purpose of life is being.
How sweet it is; how good it is.
Life is it's own reward.

Growing, glowing, knowing life,
Lifting, sifting, gifting life,
Warming, swarming life,
Electric, ecstatic life,
Increasing, never ceasing,
Life, life, life.

It breathes and grows, moves and flows.
Dancing, enhancing, romancing,
Fluctuating, participating,
Resonating, co-creating.
How sweet it is; how good it is.
Life is it's own reward.

Flexible, bendable life,
Grounding, bounding, sounding life,
Shimmering, glimmering life.
Don't take, please give.
Don't die, please live.
Life, life, life.

Let's celebrate the diverse
Life forms of the universe.
As wonders of diversity
Returns to simplicity
In spirally evolution
As billions of yearning life forms
Dance up the crystal stair.
Dance up the crystal stair.

SPIRIT GUIDE

Kristopher Xanadu
Who are you? Who are you?

I am first guide
Who sets men free.
Opens their eyes
So they can see
The newer world
That soon will be.

Kristopher Xanadu
What do you do? What do you do?

I am trickster
And fool, too.
I intrigue men,
Perplex them, true.
To wake them up
I clown around.
Confusion brings
Learning profound.

I answer call
When people seek.
I comfort them
When they do weep.
And in their quest
They pull down walls.
Between the worlds
The veil falls.

The change is here.
The time at last
When men learn fast
To live again
In worlds filled
With the teeming life
Of diversity.
You will all see.

Kristopher Xanadu
Where are you? Where are you?

I leave you now
To elsewhere be.
You do not fend
For self alone.
I always send
A higher me
To be with you
In time of change.

Kristopher Xanadu
I thank you. I thank you.

SECTION II

DIAMOND PATTERNS
ON TEXTURED GLASS

NEW BEGINNINGS

Are you and I and our fellow human beings waking up to an awareness of other worlds? Is our species evolving to a consciousness of alternate universes, parallel earths and lighter dimensions? People I consider knowledgeable say "the veils between the worlds are thinning" and "the barriers between this reality and other realities are falling".

However, is it possible humanity's expanding consciousness is providing us with evolving skills and abilities that allow us to see what was always there, but not accessible to our previously limited perceptions?

I'm not saying I have any answers. Realistically, how can anyone say they have answers when the questions keep changing so fast? But the questions keep life interesting, don't they? The following writings are not answers, only my perspectives. As the saying goes, "take it all with a grain of salt".

For part of my life, I believed the rational, logical and analytical mind was the most important thing we humans possessed. This philosophy helped me to function reasonably well as an American whose focus was mostly on the material world. I was skeptical of anything I couldn't see with my own eyes, hear with my own ears or touch with my own hands. I was wary of anything I couldn't perceive with my five senses. I considered all other experiences and happenings a product of my or someone else's imagination and without validity.

Now, after approximately twenty years on a spiritual journey, questing and seeking, I've changed my perspective. I've done research via travel, the internet, books, videotapes and attending groups and seminars. I've studied various spiritual philosophies and different religions. As helpful as my research has been, my meditations, inner work and personal experiences have been the deciding factor in changing my life view. While I still value the rational mind as a beneficial tool, I now perceive the true essence of what we are, our spirit, as the most important part of us. It is the part that will survive death. Some of my experiences have been with angels, deceased loved ones and extraterrestrials. A Time Magazine poll concluded most Americans believe in angels while a Harris Poll showed 68% of Americans believe in angels. There have been many polls taken regarding the number of Americans who believe in the existence of extraterrestrials and the results vary. A Roper Poll shows 2/3 of Americans think there are other forms of intelligent life in our universe. The same Roper Poll shows 74% are psychologically prepared for an official government announcement on the discovery of intelligent extraterrestrial life. My purpose in mentioning these polls is to emphasize that I, and the readers who have had experiences with the aforementioned beings, are not on the fringe anymore. We are becoming mainstream.

When I finally started "waking up" and becoming "more conscious", I understood that reality is very different and much larger than this agreed upon reality here on earth that does not generally include these other worldly entities. At first, my experiences were very frightening, often confusing and sometimes disorienting. There were moments when it felt as though my world was crashing around me. Slowly, I realized my confusion and fear were caused more by the massive shock to my view of reality than by the entities I encountered in various instances.

In the writings in this book, I will relate only a few of my experiences for the following reasons. We are each very unique individuals with our own distinctive viewpoints and perceive things differently. I think many spiritual and paranormal happenings are subjective, difficult to relate to others and some are meant for a particular person and no one else. Also, language fails me when I try to write about some of my experiences. And some are incorporated into my poems. Some I may include in another book.

I would like to inject a word of caution here for everyone who journeys into the spiritual and paranormal realms. Things are not necessarily what they seem. Discernment, discretion and wariness will serve you well. I would never suggest that I am beyond fear and will probably never be as long as I'm on this earth. However, fear seems to be counter productive on a spiritual journey as it may attract entities you don't want around you. There is a lot of information readily available to help you learn to protect yourself using light as well as other methods. Ask your guardian angels for assistance. Say to yourself: this is my body and mind; my space and time and I am protected. Skepticism regarding anything you hear or read, including my writings, is a healthy attitude. Cynicism, however, isn't necessarily helpful. I wrote the poem Metaphysical Blues in a cynical state of mind and only left it in the collection as an example of contrast.

"Words are tools which automatically carve concepts out of experience" (Julian Sorrell Huxley). This quote is a guide for me, although I often find words inadequate to explain spiritual and paranormal experiences. There is doubt and confusion on the spiritual path, but there is also incredible joy. I will do my best to relate here two life changing moments. The first moment came after I had finally accepted many of my encounters with other worldly beings as valid and real. The thought engulfed me that "we are not alone...we are not alone in this universe". My body, mind and spirit were filled and bursting with indescribable joy, love and gratitude. The second moment arrived later on as my acceptance continued to grow and I was suffused with a knowing that many better worlds exist where you and I will continue on. And, again, the indescribable joy enveloped me.

EXPANDING CONSCIOUSNESS

"There came a time when the risk to remain tight in the bud was more painful than the risk it took to bloom." (Anais Nin)

You and I live in a wonderfully unique time in human history. The raising of consciousness that is sweeping humanity is a momentous occurrence. It is an unprecedented opportunity for a spiritual and evolutionary leap. In my experience, the veils between the worlds are thinning. The separation between spirit and matter is less distinct than before this point in time. Angels and other worldly beings are making themselves visible to many if not all of us. It can be a time of rapid self-evolvement as we learn to use hidden abilities (intuition and precognition) and develop new skills (telepathy and healing). Of course, along with the evolving skills comes a need for self-responsibility and respect for the autonomy of others. Hopefully, these skills and abilities will serve us well as we shift ourselves into new paradigms and lighter dimensions.

<u>What is consciousness?</u> Certain scientists have proposed that it is caused by the activity of the brain which would make it a product or effect of matter. One spiritual view is that consciousness just uses the wiring of the brain through which to express itself. Other spiritual and philosophical views see consciousness as just is...a sea of energy. Still other views see it as the force behind and the substance within all matter or as "the ground of all being".

Are we then experiencing an expansion of consciousness because we are moving closer to or further into the ground of all being? Is this the source of all life? Is this God (by whatever name we choose)? My poem, Inbreath, suggests the source, God, is breathing in and recalling his creation. If each of us have a particle of consciousness, a spark of God, within us then perhaps it is our task to assist in the raising of our own consciousness.

A growing number of people in our world are thinking in wholistic terms. It is a movement away from separateness and toward wholeness. A part of this is the acceptance of the interconnection and interaction of the body, mind and spirit. Obviously, we each have a very unique body and mind and spirit; we each need to assume responsibility for the choices we make. The following should not be construed as advice for the readers; it is just a part of my personal path. I've worked hard to improve my bodily health so as to have a better vehicle for my raised consciousness. And one of the hardest things I did was to give up a nicotine cigarette addiction of many years duration. I really enjoy caffeine and sugar and carefully limit those substances. I concluded rather early in life that my genetics and my biochemistry would likely predispose me toward becoming addicted to various substances. For that reason, I never touched illegal drugs (I was sure I would like them too much). For the same reason, I was careful with alcohol and now don't drink at all. Also, I've noticed prescription medications and many over the counter medications have nasty side effects on my body and mind. Perhaps some of the readers can relate to this. For those of you who really need medications, then, of course, you should take them. For myself, I find that eating fresh, whole and organic foods as often as I can and supplementing with vitamins and minerals keeps me reasonably healthy. I strongly feel we Americans are being sold a false bill of goods on a daily basis. We are being unfairly influenced to spend our money on non-nutritional food products and various other substances that not only do we not need, but are actually bad for us.

What we ingest into our body affects our mind and our state of mind affects our spirit. It is a circular process. Many people on the spiritual path working to improve their minds and spirits are focusing on compassion, mindfulness and intention. These are huge issues and very important to our raising of consciousness. I couldn't do them justice in these writings. My hope is to whet the readers appetite to further explore these issues as well as other topics I can only touch on here. There are numerous books on Amazon.com and in bookstores which would be helpful. Wayne Dyer and Eckhardt Tolle are two authors I recommend highly.

Perhaps the reader would wish to check my Thank You Note in the front of this book for other recommended authors on the topics I cover. Hopefully, each person will find what they need to facilitate their own journey.

The massive technological change we see around us is another facet of the raising of consciousness. Any new tools humanity has can be used for the betterment or to the detriment of our species and other species. While the focus of this book is on our merging with and moving into other worlds, we are still inhabiting this world. I definitely think we should try to make this a better place as long as we're still here. To work peacefully toward a humane and rational use of our new technologies is a very worthwhile task. It is a difficult area with many ethical dilemmas.

One of the most encouraging and uplifting scenarios I've read recently regarding the raising of consciousness and humanity's dimensional shift is the one by David Wilcock (www.divinecosmos.com). He has collected scientific data that he says proves the entire solar system is heating up and/or changing dramatically. He thinks it's due to a higher energy pouring in which is also changing our DNA. Perhaps due to a repeating cosmic cycle. He seems to think the shift will happen four or five years from now and calls it ascension. Mr. Wilcock takes his many original ideas; adds some ideas that have been around a while and synthesizes the two into a very coherent theory. He envisions all of us living in better bodies in the fourth dimension.

PARANORMAL PHENOMENA

*"The important thing is to not
stop questioning." (Einstein)*

The governments of Brazil, France, England and Mexico have opened their secret UFO documents for public scrutiny. American UFO researchers speculate these actions may encourage the U.S. to open their secret UFO files as well. It has been suggested the U. S. is slowly disclosing their information about UFOs and ETs because they think a fast disclosure might cause public panic.

Despite the large number of reported sightings of flying objects and flying craft which are clearly not man made (even considering Black Ops projects) the U.S. government remains quite secretive about the whole topic. Also, large numbers of personal reports from our citizens indicating contact with extraterrestrials or abduction by extraterrestrials are ignored by our government. On July 16, 1969 the U.S. passed the "Extraterrestrial Exposure Law" (Section 1211, Title14) which makes it illegal for the public to have contact with extraterrestrials or their vehicles. Violation of this law is punishable by a fine and/ or a jail sentence. This is quite interesting considering the government is still denying the existence of ETs.

As I've written before, in the spiritual and paranormal realms things aren't necessarily what they seem. Years ago, I encountered an upright, sentient, large, non-human entity during the day time when I was wide awake. I reacted with sheer terror and left the place where I was as fast as humanly possible. As I look back, I think it was the shock/ surprise which frightened me; there may not have been any real threat present. I assumed what I saw was an ET. However, there are speculations certain non-human beings live in this world's underground caves and tunnels and are indigenous to earth. Or, perhaps they are ETs and have bases underground or even under the oceans. There have been a number of reports, some by military personnel, of UFOs being seen going into and coming out of our oceans. I have had experience with phenomena I consider to be light beings and light ships from other dimensions. In retrospect, some of them may have been time travelers. Our species is in the process of waking up and do not have <u>definitive criteria</u> with which to <u>analyze</u> the paranormal phenomena we encounter. We need to keep an open mind. A few of my past experiences have been with spheres, which I now understand is fairly common.

I am going to describe one example of my interaction with spheres, but, first, I need to digress. It is a scientifically proven fact that dogs can hear sounds in a frequency range higher than we humans. Can cats see things that are out of the range of human sight? I haven't found any scientific research to prove it. What I did find was research that says a cat's night vision and motion vision are superior to ours, while their color vision is inferior to ours. However, through the years I've heard many anecdotes from my fellow cat lovers regarding pets who seem to be seeing things their humans don't see. As well as anecdotes regarding telepathy with their pets. I think a survey of cat lovers would validate the existence of these skills in certain cats. Now, my example. My much loved golden cat, who has now passed on, used to telepath to me with pictures. I became certain of this when I was away from home one night. I kept getting pictures of him standing outside my front door yowling. Since he was an indoor cat, I discounted the pictures. The next day I phoned home to the person who was taking care of him. She said he evidently ran outside when she wasn't looking and had been out in the cold and dark for hours. After that experience, I paid more attention to my cat when he would quickly jump up from resting and look up in the air, eyes wide with awe. He never seemed scared, but appeared to be thinking, "Wow, that's interesting". I would think to him, "Show me a picture of what you see". I would receive pictures of typical angels; women with long white robes and wings. After years of this, it occurred to me that my mind and cultural bias might be filtering what he was sending. I decided I would blank my mind as much as possible to get a more accurate picture. After that decision, I received pictures of translucent, golden globes a little smaller than soccer balls. It seemed to me there was always a slight ringing as well as pleasant feelings accompanying these incidents. I think they were benevolent light beings who may very well be the same as angels.

Another example: About thirteen years ago I was in the middle of my quest for knowledge. It was about 11:00 p.m. and I was sitting in my living room with my golden cat on my lap. I was feeling a little down, not depressed, just discouraged about the state of the world and life in general. Suddenly, there was the sound of a helicopter over my house. It became very loud as though it was going to crash through my living room ceiling. I picked up my cat and decided to get out of there. I went through the dining room and outside onto the deck. For the record, I was wide awake, had not been asleep, was sober and straight, had not taken any prescription drugs or over the counter medications. I know precisely what happened and what I saw.

On the deck I stood and stared. To the northwest just above a group of trees were two gigantic orange/red globes. The larger one was about the size of a football field; the other one was slightly smaller. Their surfaces were roiling and swirling with various shades of orange, ranging from a milky pale orange to an almost red/orange. I felt no fear, but stood there stupefied.

I said out loud, "Those are ships".

Immediately, I heard in my head, "We've come to give you hope".

With the telepathy came a knowing that this was a friend of mine from the future, with a mate, who had come back to assist me in my process of waking up. Then, a small, dull gray, unmarked airplane flew from the south straight toward the globes. Immediately, the smaller globe blinked twice, very fast. Next, the larger globe blinked twice, very fast. The smaller one moved at tremendous speed straight to the north and stopped. The larger one followed and stopped. The smaller one blinked twice; the larger one blinked twice. The smaller one moved at incredible speed to the east and vanished. The larger one did the same. I stood on the deck watching as the small plane flew on for awhile. Then it banked, turned and flew back the way it had come.

At the time this incident occurred, I had no information about spheres or colored globes. And very little understanding of telepathy. I decided to accept this unusual happening as another mystery to be carefully considered. I wanted it to be exactly what it seemed to be. Many years have passed. Now, I think the incident was what it seemed to be.

My guess is the globes projected the helicopter sound to get me out onto the deck. I don't know what type of airplane flew toward the globes or whether it was military or civilian. Because of the advanced technology the globes exhibited, I assume they left so as to not interfere with an airplane in the third dimension or, perhaps, from their past. In the last few years there is a tremendous amount of information on the internet about colored globes and spheres, but I have never read or heard anything exactly matching my experience. Recently, on the internet are suggestions that our government uses technology to create plasma balls in the sky to simulate UFOs and confuse people. This may be true or not. However, I feel pretty sure those plasma balls weren't around thirteen years ago. And, if they were, I'm pretty sure they couldn't have sent me telepathy and information of their origins or exhibited the technology I saw.

Quite a number of paranormal experiencers, including me, accept that certain dreams are not just dreams, but are contacts with other worldly beings. I have many memories of such contacts. Most of the time, the beings appear to be ETs. Sometimes angels. My memories are of being taught various things; being given various lessons. Often, I'm sitting in a classroom with other humans. In one dream contact, I was flying through the air with two small angels on either side of me holding my hands.

I asked, "Where are we going"?

They answered, "We're going to take you into the Great Light".

I saw just ahead of us a large, beautiful, golden light. I felt fear and said, "No, no, no."

I jerked awake and sat up in bed. I had said no because I feared losing myself if I flew into the Great Light. I am not an especially brave experiencer. Perhaps I passed up what would have been a transformative moment. However, I think we can only do what our level of spiritual development allows us to do.

Some of my dream contacts have been with ETs who are not very pretty, but they are teaching me things and I seem to be comfortable with them in that context. Perhaps we humans don't look very pretty to them either. I think there are good and bad ETs as there are good and bad humans. I've had some very frightening contact experiences both in the wide awake state and the dream state. As the years unfold, some of the fear has gone away. Hopefully, an expanding consciousness will lessen fear of the unknown for all of us.

Humor has helped me to survive a mysterious and rapidly changing world. I have laughed at and expressed smart aleck remarks to many entities I've encountered. One told me he/they understood it was my defense mechanism, but it still stung them. I don't do it as much anymore. However, I do maintain we have a right to make our own choices. I do maintain this is my body and mind; my space and time. I am the one here on earth in the third dimension and will live this life as I see fit. At this point in time, I've never been given advice or even suggestions by beings from other realms or other realities. If I ever do, I will be very wary of it.

SPIRITUALITY & SCIENCE

*"Miracles do not , in fact, break the
laws of nature." (C. S. Lewis)*

I wrote the poem Quarks after studying the fascinating topic of the merging of spirituality and science. For some time science and spirituality have been seen as two completely separate things. Now, they seem to be coming together. There is growing recognition that the underlying concepts of both may be the same. The differences may be in the terms and phrases used for the description of each.

Due to the efforts of a number of renouned physicists the theories of quantum physics were developed around 1900. The applicable equations and the terms of quantum mechanics were presented in 1924 or 1925. There have been many good books written by physicists, other scientists and educated lay persons favorably comparing the principles of quantum physics to the attributes of spirituality and mysticism. They write that quantum physics encompasses the super string theory which suggests ten or twelve dimensions other than this one. Perhaps, even, a multiplicity of other dimensions. Might this correspond to some spiritual beliefs regarding many other worlds after this one? Quantum physics includes the unified field theory which suggests everyone and everything is interrelated and interconnected. Might this correspond to spiritual beliefs of the Oneness of all life? One author even writes about what he sees as a similarity between photons and angels. Two worthwhile books are

The Tao of Physics (Fritjof Capra) and The Self Aware Universe (Amit Goswami).

David Bohm (1917-94) was a highly respected quantum physicist. Bohm proposed that the material world we see around us is the explicate order. Higher dimensions are the implicate order. And even higher dimensions are the super implicate order. He thought the implicate order includes the explicate order and was the totality of all that was, is and will be. Essentially a sea of energy...a sea of consciousness which effects and forms the material world. And the material world feeds information back to the sea of consciousness. He saw this as a dynamic interconnectedness of all that is. There are obvious spiritual corollaries in his theories. Bohm also thought everything works on a holographic model. As the whole of something contains all of it's parts, each part contains the whole. Certain spiritual philosophies see a spark, a particle, of All That Is in every one and everything.

I am encouraged by thinkers who are connecting the concepts of science and spirituality. Certain modern visionaries see a general movement in our world from separateness back to wholeness in many areas of life.

OUT OF BODY & MULTIDIMENSIONALITY

"Death, by itself, is nothing. But we
fear to be we know not what; we
know not where." (John Dryden)

There is a theory that every human being in the world leaves their body every night when they sleep and even when they nap during the day. Of course, it's only a theory. Recent statistics say one out of every ten Americans have reported having had an out of body experience (OBE) <u>while awake</u>. This seems to me to be another facet of the expanding consciousness of our species.

There are different opinions as to what constitutes an out of body experience. What goes out of our body? Is it our mind? Our spirit? Our light body? Is it all of these? I've heard certain remote viewers say they are out of body when they practice their skills. Other remote viewers disagree and say they only project their minds and do not leave their bodies. Author Jim Marrs has a new book entitled PSI Spies about remote viewing. It's very revealing. There is some agreement that meditation does not constitute an out of body experience unless the person is in a very deep, altered state. There is considerable agreement the near death experience (NDE) is an out of body occurrence. As with other paranormal phenomena we do not, yet, have definitive criteria with which to analyze the process.

As far as new frontiers and the challenges they present,

I think out of body travel is at the top of the list. In order to function in our bodies in this third dimension, we've needed to focus here and stay grounded. We've needed to forget other dimensions, parallel worlds and past lives. Now, we are being asked to let go of that narrow, limited focus and face the challenges of the unknown. A tough assignment.

William Buhlman wrote, "When I am asked, why out of body exploration, my response is simple. I want to know the answers for myself." Mr. Buhlman's books on OBEs are the very best of the many I've read on this topic. He makes a complicated subject understandable and writes in a very readable style.

As far as the nuts and bolts of how to leave your body and how to navigate in other worlds Mr. Buhlman's books are excellent. Of course, there are other authors who are good in this area as well. As far as whether or not an individual should or should not explore this subject; it is for each one to decide. If a person is having serious mental, psychological or emotional issues, perhaps they need to work on those problems for the present and avoid this area.

Years ago I experimented with the techniques for going out of body while awake. I couldn't do it. I was trying too hard and, of course, that doesn't work. Relaxing enough to go into an altered state may work. Then, I realized it wasn't a skill that was important for me. Although, at the time, I did have a dream where I was floating by the ceiling in my den. A while after that I had an unusual experience. I found myself in complete darkness. I could hear snoring and then knew I was next to my sleeping body.

Immediately, I was in my body and awake. Years later I read that when we're very close to our body it's dark and we have to move further away to have vision. Perhaps this doesn't apply to everyone, but seemed to apply to me.

As of this writing, I do not have voluntary control over leaving my body and do not feel the need of that. What has been happening to me through the years are a multitude of experiences when I'm in a hypnagogic state...just before falling asleep. I'm definitely in a very relaxed, altered state, but not quite asleep. I have a good imagination, but could not possibly imagine the amazing worlds I find myself in. Nor could I imagine the unusual, but seemingly safe, entities I meet. There are people who say the experiences that happen during the hypnagogic state do not constitute OBEs. I disagree. I seem to be out of my body. I do experience symptoms such as a tugging at the top of my head or on my abdomen when leaving my body. Also, I hear a whooshing, ringing or clanging when moving out of my body. On some occasions I would find myself in nasty situations or with scary seeming entities. I would think, "I'm out of here", would feel my body jerk and would be back in it. Often, in pleasant situations, I would strive to stay awake. I could only stay awake and/or consciously out of body for a short time.

I asked my spirit guides (gaurdian angels) why I couldn't sustain the out of body experiences. This is what they told me, via telepathy. Before I came to this third dimensional, material world I charged them with keeping me here until I completed certain work. They cannot let me stay long in other worlds as I may forget my reasons for being here and not come back.

Because of the brevity of the experiences, my out of body travel has been limited. Even with that, I am 100% convinced we survive the shedding of the body which we call death and live on in other worlds. This leads me to accept greater responsibility for my thoughts and actions. It encourages me to direct my own spiritual evolvement.

It seems to me humanity is in the process of growing up. I think we've been in the adolescent stage of development using our five senses to function in the material world for a long time. Now, we are growing up, opening up to more expansive ways of being. On my spiritual journey I've muttered to myself many times "grow up, grow up...it's time to grow up".

As I said previously, I am certain we, our essence, our spirit, survives death to go into other worlds. I am equally certain we can go to a world or worlds of our own choosing. In this dimension our thoughts create our reality to some degree. A person thinks about a unique and beautiful piece of furniture. Then, the person designs it and has it built. The thought had to come first. I'm sure the same applies in lighter dimensions, except our thoughts manifest much faster. Why? Because the lighter dimensions are vibrating faster. I think we can plan what kind of a world we want to go to from here. Perhaps it will help if we envision it; write about it and even speak out loud about it. Also, my personal experience has convinced me we can move ourselves out of undesirable worlds with our thoughts.

Multidimensionality is a word I read about fifteen years ago. The author wrote that we all have many other parts of ourselves in many other dimensions. At the time I couldn't quite get my mind around the idea. I have long accepted the premise there is a oneness which encompasses everyone and everything. And that everyone and everything are interconnected. Perhaps there are beings who are considered oversouls who guide many souls and not necessarily only humans.

Today, the ideas from quantum physics are spreading rapidly and the theory of many dimensions is becoming accepted. Now, the idea of multidimensionality seems more reasonable to me. During my hypnagogic and hypnopompic (waking from sleep, but not fully awake) states I've met a number of entities and beings who have told me they are parts of me in other dimensions. None of them were human. I have no particular reason to doubt them. They did not give me advice, ask anything of me or tell me to do anything. The only apparent purpose for their brief visits seemed to be to offer me an opportunity to expand my perception of reality.

It's likely almost everyone has heard the theory of parallel earths or parallel universes. There are some popular movies and books on this subject. It's been suggested the parallel earths branch off from each other. I've had three separate experiences which seem to coincide with this theory. When relating any of my unusual experiences, I will be straight forward and not embellish or exaggerate in any way. However, these happenings were not as clear cut as some others. Each of these experiences were with a different human female; each looked somewhat like me and somewhat like each other. They each claimed we were different versions of each other on parallel earths. Their lives and situations in their worlds were very different than mine here. One visit occurred a few years ago, during the day, when I was sitting and reading. I was relaxed, but not anywhere near sleep. Suddenly, a woman appeared. I could see her clearly, in color and in details of dress. Although, she was not quite as clear and substantial as you and I would be to each other. We conversed telepathically and she said she slipped in here because her life was in immediate danger in her world. Then she disappeared. A second visit occurred recently. Again, it was daytime and I was relaxed but not anywhere near sleep. Surprisingly, I found myself in an very unusual and unfamiliar apartment with a woman who looked something like me. She telepathed to me she had called me there because she wanted to come back with me. I returned to awareness here. I assumed she came back with me; I can't be sure. The third visit happened quite a few years ago. I was coming awake (hypnopompic state), but felt fully awake and was sitting up in bed. A woman appeared beside me. She telepathed to me she came from a world even more violent than this one and was about to be killed. So, she slipped in here to avoid it. She also disappeared. There was more conversation and more details than I'm reporting here, but they don't seem relevant at this time.

Now, it gets even a little more woo-woo. I'm not certain, but I think these women stayed in this world in some form, either in conciousness or a light body or in a regular body. All three of them told me the third dimension will shut down soon and everyone will be moved into lighter worlds. None of them could tell me how soon or how it was going to happen. They all informed me they were supposed to be on this earth when it occurred as this earth is an access point (their words). This is a little nebulous, but I got the impression our world is an inter-dimensional vortex. Personally, I didn't think "the third dimension shutting down" was big news. After all, the third dimension will definitely shut down for each of us when we shed our body and move on. To me, neither of these occurrences mean death or endings, but mean only change, transformation and new beginnings. I've had very strong feelings I'm supposed to include these experiences with the three women even at the risk of ridicule or being thought bonkers. The reason may be that these types of occurrences will be happening to more and more people. If so, some people will have this information and not think they're going bonkers. Acquaintances who've read this material for me before publication suggested I include a few personal facts so as to lend more credibility to my writings. I've never been diagnosed with a mental illness, spent time in a mental hospital or a psych ward. I've never been arrested or spent time in jail. Please don't think I'm being self-righteous. While I try to weigh consequences before I act, I have occasionally done some foolish and even stupid things. It is partly due to dumb luck and my guardian angels that I haven't gotten into trouble. I'm a work in progress. Perhaps some of the readers can relate to this.

Near death experiences (NDEs) are being reported, discussed, researched and accepted by many people as valid. It is suggested these experiences are occurring more often than in past years because of the very effective resusitation techniques of modern medicine. We are reviving quite a few people who were considered dead. The commonality of most, not all, reported NDEs are; leaving the body, going through a tunnel, meeting deceased loved ones, being enveloped in feelings of love, joy and belonging and having a life review. There are many worthwhile books and websites available on this topic. The personal reports of NDEs are encouraging and inspiring. They offer us hope for the continuation of our consciousness.

COMPLETION & GRADUATION

*"I existed from all eternity and I am here.
And I shall exist till the end of time, for my
being has no end." (Kahlil Gibran)*

There are various facets to the massive changes we see all around us. The pace of technological change is astonishing. The raising of consciousness of our species may be an increase in intelligence. It may be a change in our DNA as well as a spiritual transformation. It may be all three.

Is this a time of graduation for our species? Is this a time of completion of many ancient cycles? Are there new light and new energy streaming in from the great central sun? Are we seeing the transmutation of earth with everyone and everything on it into a less dense state of being? Is the third dimension completely shutting down? There are authors that write some or all of the above things are happening.

It can be confusing. However, it seems to me there is one thing we can all be certain about. At some point, we will all leave this world. Perhaps by shedding our bodies in death. Perhaps by ascension with our bodies. Perhaps by the movement of earth with everyone and everything on it into a lighter dimension. The commonality here is they all result in our shifting into a lighter dimension. Before we further explore leaving the earth, let's look at how we may have come to be here.

Our species has always questioned our origins. The creationists credit a Creator with intelligent design. The evolutionists credit nature with gradually developing one species from another. There is an additional theory called intervention. This theory credits a technologically advanced race or species with genetically engineering earth's hominids to create homo sapiens. Zecharia Sitchin was one author, among others, who suggested this.

I don't understand the serious disagreements between creationists and evolutionists. To me, they are both reasonable and complement each other. Perhaps the Creator instructed nature to gradually evolve and unfold the creation. Isn't that intelligent design? I do understand the resistance to the theory of intervention. We humans don't like the idea of a technologically superior race or species manipulating us, genetically or otherwise. However, there seems to be some evidence to support this theory. So, isn't it possible the Creator instructed his more evolved creations to assist in the creative process? Isn't this, also, intelligent design? I try to think in an inclusive manor and perceive an ongoing flow of life and creation that encompasses all three theories.

A few days ago I heard someone giving a speech say life on planet earth is an experiment where light beings volunteered to enter animal bodies. I listened carefully but didn't hear him offer any reason for the experiment. If we could assume for the moment this is true, perhaps the purpose is to lighten up and evolve the animal bodies. Some call it evolution. Some call it God. I call it both. I also call it the transmutation of matter or even ascension. There are a number of people on earth who are working diligently at lightening up their bodies enough to ascend in the body. I've personally met a few of them. They believe that is their task in this lifetime. It's possible they are a little further along the evolutionary ladder than most of us. Or is it Jacob's ladder?

Why is there so much suffering and misery and continuation of wars on planet earth? Why are we humans so inhumane to each other and to other species? I don't know. Certain people lay it to free will. Some people say this definitely is an experiment in matter and duality and it isn't working. And other people say we have moved too far away from the Prime Creator. The separation is too great; the territory too dark and dense. And great darkness and density make change for the better very, very difficult.

If, like me, you occasionally become discouraged with the questions and the questing, then pull back and take care of yourself. Rest and find recreation. Just making a living, paying the bills, putting food on the table and mowing the lawn can be challenging in an increasely complicated world. But, don't forget to be very, very grateful if you can make a living, pay the bills and put food on the table and that you have a lawn to mow.

Aren't we a little like cats in that our curiosity is always with us? After we rest it leads us back to the questions and the quest.

My past study of the world's major religions (Judaism, Christianity, Islam, Hinduism and Buddhism) was interesting and a little confusing. My present research on the world's major religions has been the same. There are many sects within the various religions...each sect having somewhat different beliefs from the other sects. However, all the religions I have studied have stories/myths about cycles of creation, destruction and creation again. And, of course, the sects within the religions have varied predictions about when and how these cycles will occur.

While there are end of the world scenarios currently circulating in various countries and cultures, I choose to mention only those being talked about and written about here in America. Obviously, these are the ones I'm most familiar with. There are philosophers and visionaries who suggest the earth is a school house for learning lessons. Some of them suggest the lessons have become too harsh and it's time to close the school. It's time to graduate. Perhaps that is one of the reasons there are so many end of the world predictions making the rounds. It's true there have been these predictions throughout history. But, today, many people seem to be yearning for the end... hoping for the apocalypse. And expecting it soon.

Let's look at some of the scenarios.

> The earth itself will undergo a dramatic pole shift and most of humanity will be wiped out. The humans who survive will be living in primitive societies.

> The Mayan calendar ends on December 21, 2012 and the world as we know it ends also. Further predictions propose a dimensional shift for everyone.

> Certain Christians are hoping Jesus will rapture them off of the planet before a terrible tribulation begins.

Other Christians are expecting Jesus to return and usher in 1,000 years of peace on planet earth.

One visionary sees the third dimension completely shutting down. Everyone will move into the fifth dimension.

Another visionary sees mother earth giving birth and pushing the new earth into a lighter world with only enlightened humans on it.

Some New Agers are hoping the ETs will lift them off of the planet and into space ships before cataclysmic happenings (a pole shift?) here on earth.

Certain Native Americans say everything is ending here and we will all move into the Fifth world. They also use the phrase, "this dream is ending; it's time to dream a new dream".

New Thought philosophers propose that the current expansion of consciousness of humanity will literally raise our vibration, lift us up and shift us all into a lighter dimension...a better world.

I don't know if we are currently living in the end times. I do think we are in a very important juncture in human history. And a time of unprecedented change and unprecedented possibilities.

It helps me to view change as a constant. As an ongoing process with which we live every day. I think all of life is under the pressure of evolution; the pressure to become more than what it already is. It has been suggested the human body is a cocoon. And soon we will shed it for our butterfly stage...our light body.

With the vast amount of conflicting information available to us, how can we know what is true? Perhaps we each need to get in touch with our own truths. Our inner truths. Knowing comes in different ways. Perhaps through meditation or prayer. Perhaps through reclaiming our intuition. Perhaps through personal experiences. The pathway of expanded consciousness and spirituality is often an individual journey.

In my heart, I feel sure the most important lesson we're supposed to learn while on planet earth is to love each other and the Creator. And to leave fear behind as we choose love. I strongly feel humanity will be moving into places in space and time where these lessons will be easier to learn. Places in space and time where love will surround us; where love is the ground of being.

SECTION III

DIAMOND PATTERNS
ON TEXTURED GLASS

CHANGE

Come on out of the closet.
Quit sitting there in the dark.
Everything is changing,
Come on...do your part.

The costume party is over.
Let's take off the mask.
Time for learning is past;
Time to do your task.
When any one of you
Remembers your true name,
It will facilitate
The spirit of the change.

I listened carefully
And the wings of change
Flew my name to me
Through corridors of time.
Then it was mine.
I am Kristar. I am Kristar.
I help bring the changes in.
I help bring the changes in.

It's springtime in the world;
Be glad that you're here.
Time to grow new things;
Perhaps you'll grow some wings.
As we crystallize this rock,

Turn this planet to a star.
Then we'll all lift up,
Lift up, lift up with a star.

When you listen well
You'll hear your star name
And will participate
In the spirit of the change.
Let's crystallize this rock,
Turn this planet to a star.
Then we'll all lift up,
Lift up, lift up with a star.

METAPHYSICAL BLUES

I'm sick of doing hard time on planet earth.
I want to go home to the sky.
I'm doing hard time on planet earth
And don't know the reason why.
Can't remember my crime.
Why am I doing the time?
They say we create our own reality.
I think that's a mock.
I want off of this rock.
How do I get off of this rock?

This is a prison planet.
There was never any doubt.
I want to see the warden.
I want to find out
If I can get a parole
And still save my soul.
I thought compassion was a virtue.
Now I wonder if that's true.
From people's suffering, I can't hide.
Pain takes a toll; it's tearing up my soul.

Hope all this serves some cosmic plan,
"Cause I'm not coming here again.
Can't drink the water; can't eat the food.
They say it's for some ultimate good.
Beginning to feel, I want a new deal.
Can't we reshuffle the deck?
Can't we reroll the dice?

Did we truly know the price
We would have to pay
When we came here from far away?

Don't believe I did this to myself.
Create your own reality's a mock!
How do I get off of this rock?
I'm sick of doing hard time on planet earth
And don't know the reason why.
I'm sick of doing hard time on planet earth
And want to go home to the sky.
Is there a password I forgot
To get myself off of this rock?

INTUITION

Those senses beyond the common five
Were long clouded and shrouded by fear.
The whispering, small voice inside of us,
In this time of change, is coming clear.

Survival of the fittest was our path.
Now moving in a higher evolution
Of awareness and expanded consciousness
Does develop the sense of intuition.

The higher self comes down to befriend us.
Streams of living truth come our way.
Assistance and support are fully present.
Insights, new perceptions here to stay.

Altruism replaces baser instincts
And views with compassion all we see.
A comprehension beyond the physical
Shows non-judgmental love is the key.

GREATEST WEALTH

Look at what they did to poor Moses.
Forty years in the desert's not fun.
Look at what they did to poor Jesus.
A cross is not a prize to be won.
An urge to be a prophet
Is detrimental to your health.
If you talk to God, keep it to yourself.
Inner peace and harmony is your greatest wealth.

Look at what they did to King Arthur.
He had a concept good and true.
Lost his queen to another;
Lost his round table, too.
Look at what they did to Kennedy.
He founded a new Camelot.
Gave his best for the country free.
We cried when the poor man was shot.

So if you're favored by the gods,
Think long and carefully.
What happens to favorites isn't nice.
Better lead yourself to be free.
So if you talk to God, don't let it be known.
They might lock you in; say your mind has flown.
Everyone of us is learning fast.
Perhaps the time for prophets is past.

Thank you...thank you...Moses.
Thank you...thank you...Jesus.
Thank you, brothers, brave and true
For everything you went through.
But we will talk to God
And find our own release.
We will each talk to God
And seek our inner peace.

If we talk to God
We'll keep it to our self.
Inner peace and harmony
Is our greatest wealth.

GAIA

Gaia, my mother, Gaia, my earth,
This naked ape thanks you for giving her birth.
It's time to replenish; it's time to renew.
Put the seed into the ground, stomp it down, all around.
  Gonna do the naked ape dance.
  Gonna do the naked ape dance.
    In freedom now
    In freedom now
    In freedom now

To the starlight of my fathers,
The fertile fields of my mothers,
I pay homage now. I give the honor bow.
I give thanks to bring union now.
In communion now; there's union now.
  Gonna do the naked dance.
  Gonna do the naked dance.
    In freedom now
    In freedom now
    In freedom now

Why did the dinosaurs go away?
Wonder what they look like today?
Maybe they'll come back to play.
Let's have respect for all forms of life.
Let's heal the earth and end the strife.

Gonna do the naked ape dance.
Gonna do the naked ape dance.
   In freedom now
   In freedom now
   In freedom now

In the fields of love is plenty of food
To feed the earth's children. All of it good.
Time to move into the light.
Time to join the day and the night.
In union now, there's communion now.
   Gonna do the naked ape dance.
   Gonna do the naked ape dance.
      In freedom now
      In freedom now
      In freedom now.

KUNDALINI

Kundalini rising,
Snaking up the spine.
Knowing comes so easy;
Wisdom's yours and mine.
Secrets of the universe
Always hidden from us
Are for the having now.
The truth is with us now.
Comes the energy
Creative energy
  Juices flowing free
  Juices flowing free

Comes the fever hot.
The burning doesn't stop.
In our solar plexus
Is a red hot sun.
Transmutation fever
Is not a lot of fun.
All those aches and flushes
Can feel like brushes
With the specter of death.
Drink lots of water
  To be fever free
  To be fever free

The dreamers are awake
To knowledge replicate.

Essential to the moment
Comes the wisdom true.
Purpose of the universe
Is much clearer too.
Strangeness turns to love.
Message from above.
Use that energy
Creative energy
  In the service of love
  In the service of love

LAW OF GRACE

The law of karma went away;
The law of grace is here to stay.
All past debts repaid today.
Let all sorrows fall away.
Joy floods through, generations renew,
There's now forgiveness bright.
Grace makes the karma right.

The past won't last; it's going fast.
The people want to go home.
They've been long enough in the clay.
The people want to go home;
They claim their freedom today.

There are parts of you and parts of me
That reach out hands from darker places
Wanting to be free.
They bring us many graces
As the light shines on their faces.
As we change dark to light;
As love illuminates the night.

The past won't last; it's going fast.
The people want to go home.
They've been long enough in the clay.
The people want to go home;
They claim their freedom today.

Grace is the honey of the soul;
It sweetens and makes us whole.
It may get darker still,
So push away the fear
Until the tunnel opens clear.
Then we'll funnel up the tunnel
All the years full of fears.

The past won't last; it's going fast.
The people want to go home.
They've been long enough in the clay.
The people want to go home;
They claim their freedom today.

Moses led his people free;
Now another march through time.
A higher vibration is the key.
Lighter tones are just fine.
Let's help each other on the way.
We're tired of bondage in the clay.
Let's claim our freedom today.

IN THE LIGHT

I will swim like a dolphin in a sea of love.
I will glide like a seagull in the sky above.
I will play like a child in the springtime of life.
I will lift into joy far above the strife.
In the light, in the light,
In the living light.

The golden light is a part of me.
It leads me where I need to be.
There are golden cities in the air.
We'll be there...we'll be there.
Without fear, without fear,
Let the fear fall away.

I will dance like a sunbeam high in the sky.
I will float like a cloud in the blue bye and bye.
I will sing and dance and swing and sway.
I will move my body in a rhythmic way.
In the light, in the light,
In the living light.

The golden age is here to stay.
It brings us to a brighter day.
I will live in the light.
I will love in the light.
Without fear, without fear,
Let the fear fall away.

I will breathe in the light.
I will walk in the light.
I will know who I AM.
I will be who I AM.
I will live in the love of the light.

CHRYSALIS

Spirit wrapped

In human body;

Sheds it soon